W9-DEV-224

First Questions and Answers about **Nature**

Why Is the Grass Green?

TIME LIFE *for* Children®

ALEXANDRIA, VIRGINIA

Contents

Why is the grass green?

Grass and leaves are green because they have something green inside them. This green stuff is called chlorophyll. Chlorophyll is like a tiny kitchen inside every leaf! It helps turn sunlight and water into food for the plant.

Quick! Count how many different green plants you see before I'm blown awa-a-a-y!

Why do dandelions get fuzzy?

Dandelions get fuzzy to make new flowers! Those fuzzy heads are made of silky grayish-white threads with a dandelion seed at the bottom. A breeze pulls the seeds off the flower. The threads act like a feathery parachute for each seed. The parachutes carry the seeds far away on the wind. New dandelions can grow from the seeds wherever they land.

Try it!
Pick a fuzzy dandelion and blow on it. Watch the seeds fly away!

How does a dandelion grow from a seed?

My friends love flowers.

Once a seed lands in the soft dirt, it soaks up water, and its shell cracks.

Small roots grow from the seed and into the earth. The roots suck up water from the soil like straws.

Next a small green shoot appears. This will be the flower's stem! It needs a lot of water and sun to grow. It gets taller and taller. Leaves grow from the stem.

A tiny bud appears, and then a bright yellow dandelion blooms!

Finally, the dandelion becomes a puff ball, and its seeds are carried far away to make new dandelions.

Did you know?
Almost all plants—from the tiniest flowers to the biggest trees—grow from seeds!

9

Why do bees buzz around flowers?

Because the bees are hungry! Flowers have things bees need to eat. One is nectar. Nectar is a sweet liquid in flowers that bees use to make honey. Flowers that smell sweet and have bright colors often have a lot of nectar, so bees like them best.

Did you know?
Butterflies also drink flower nectar, and they love sweet-smelling flowers!

Why do roses have thorns?

Animals and birds like to come close to roses because they smell so good. Sharp thorns help keep the roses from being crushed or eaten. Anyone who gets too close will get pricked.

13

Are flowers alive?

All plants—from trees and bushes to grass and flowers—are alive. Like all living things, they grow bigger. And they need water and food. They drink water through their roots, and their green chlorophyll makes their food.

How do birds build nests?

Different kinds of birds make their nests in different ways. Many birds weave their nests out of twigs, leaves, grass, feathers, string, and anything else they can pick up. Some birds use mud to make the walls strong. But not all birds build nests. Woodpeckers and owls make their nests in holes in trees.

Did you know?
Many birds build their nests high in trees to stay safe from their enemies down on the ground.

Why do birds sing different songs?

Because they have so much to tell one another! Father birds sing songs to mother birds. Mother birds chirp to their babies when danger is near. Baby birds peep to their mother when they are hungry. Birds fighting over a worm squawk and cackle. Other sounds help bird families stay together and keep outsiders away.

Try it!

Different kinds of birds make different sounds. A dove coos, a crow caws, and an owl says "Who!" Listen to all the bird songs in your yard or neighborhood park. Try to see which birds are making each sound.

19

How do birds fly?

Birds are specially made for flying. First, birds are very strong. They have to be strong to flap their wings hard enough to lift them off the ground. Also, birds' bones are hollow, so they don't weigh very much. Finally, birds are covered with feathers. The feathers push against the air as birds flap their wings and lift them up into the sky.

Did you know?

Most baby birds don't have feathers when they first hatch. In a few weeks, though, they grow feathers and start to learn to fly.

Why do some trees look smooth and some trees look rough?

All trees are covered with a kind of skin called bark. Different kinds of trees have different kinds of bark. Most trees have smooth bark when they're young. But as a tree gets bigger, the tree trunk gets fatter. The growing part inside pushes the bark out. On many trees, the bark cracks because it can't stretch. The cracks make the bark rough.

There's nothing better than a picnic on a warm summer day.

Where are all those ants going?

Those worker ants are bringing home supper! Ants live in underground nests with lots of different rooms connected by tunnels. The ant queen stays in one room. She's the biggest ant in the nest and the mother of all the workers. They bring her food and keep her clean. In other rooms, workers rest, take care of baby ants, and store food. Thousands of ants may live in one nest!

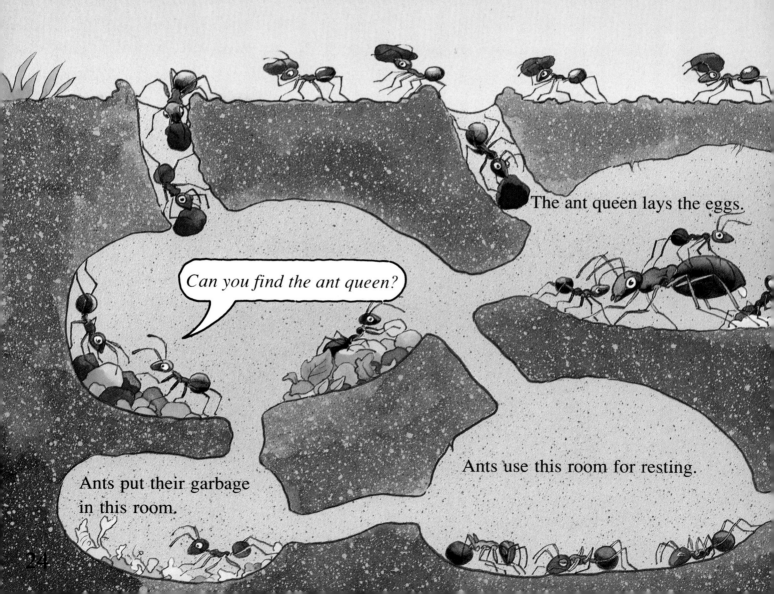

The ant queen lays the eggs.

Can you find the ant queen?

Ants put their garbage in this room.

Ants use this room for resting.

Wormlike creatures, called larvae,
hatch from the eggs.

The larvae spin cocoons.
Several weeks later, baby ants
come out of the cocoons.

Where do animals go when it rains?

Some animals don't mind the rain a bit! But if it is raining really hard, others may try to hide from the rain and stay dry.

Beavers can stay outside in the rain because their fur is like a raincoat. It keeps the water out.

Ducks' feathers are like beavers' fur. Ducks can stay out in the rain, too.

Squirrels hide on leafy branches or in their nests in the tops of trees.

Deer curl up under bushes.

Rabbits jump into empty skunk or woodchuck holes or hide under bushes.

When it rains, I hide under a leaf. It's like a big umbrella.

Why do we see more worms after it rains?

Worms live in underground tunnels that they dig. But when it rains, their holes fill with water, so they have to leave. And when they get above ground, they'd better watch out. Robins love to eat worms!

Did you know?
Worms eat mostly dirt and leaves.

Why are there seashells in my garden?

Not all shells are seashells. And not all shells are at the seashore. Snails, who live in shells, can be found almost anywhere. They live in ponds and streams, your backyard, *and* the ocean.

Did you know?

A slug is a kind of snail that doesn't have a shell. Snails and slugs both move very slo-o-owly.

Snails and slugs leave a slimy trail everywhere they go! The slime helps them hold on to things as they climb.

Where do butterflies come from?

A butterfly begins its life as an egg laid by its mother.

Several days later, the egg hatches into a caterpillar.

The caterpillar eats leaves and grows.

It sheds its skin as it gets bigger. A new skin is underneath.

Then it hangs from a plant
and spins a cocoon. The cocoon
covers the whole caterpillar.

The caterpillar stays inside
this cocoon for a few weeks.
Then it breaks out as . . .

a beautiful butterfly!

Why do leaves change color in the fall?

Leaves don't really change to new colors, they just lose their green color. Most leaves have yellow or orange or red in them already. But in spring and summer there's so much green from the chlorophyll that it hides the leaves' other colors. In the fall, the green chlorophyll goes away. Then we can see the other beautiful colors that were there all the time!

This leaf is beginning to look like me!

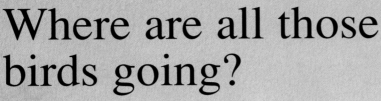

Where are all those birds going?

They're going where it's warmer now that winter is coming. Birds need food all year. In warmer places there's plenty to eat, even in the winter. Birds that fly away in the fall come back again in the spring. Some birds fly together in the shape of a sideways letter V.

Not all birds fly to warmer places in the winter. Some birds don't mind the cold if they can find enough to eat.

Try it!

Make a pine-cone feeder for winter birds in your neighborhood. With an adult's help, find a big pine cone and spread creamy peanut butter on all of its cracks and edges. Roll the gooey pine cone in birdseed, tie a string to the top, and hang it from a high branch.

37

Do trees die in the winter?

Trees don't die in the winter, even though they might look like they do. Trees that lose their leaves in the fall are still alive. In the warm spring, the trees will make new leaves and grow bigger in the bright summer sun.

Did you know?

Trees do die—of old age, disease, or even from a fire or a lightning bolt. A dead tree doesn't grow new leaves, and it doesn't get any bigger. Over time, dead trees lose their branches and become rotten logs.

What is a mushroom?

A mushroom is a kind of plant. Mushrooms often grow on dead plants, such as rotten logs or piles of leaves. Mushrooms aren't green, but they come in a lot of other colors, and in all shapes and sizes. Some even have polka dots!

Did you know?

People and animals like to eat mushrooms. But they have to be careful. Some mushrooms are poisonous. So don't ever eat a mushroom that you find outside. It could be poisonous and make you very sick.

Why do some trees stay green in the winter?

Pine trees have green needles all year long. Pine needles are leaves that are very sharp and pointy! They don't mind the cold as much as other kinds of leaves, so they don't all drop off in the fall.

Pine trees and some other trees and bushes lose leaves—or needles—a few at a time all year long. New ones keep growing in, so it's hard to tell any leaves ever fell off at all.

Did you know?

A pine cone is a case for a pine tree's seeds. Pine cones have scales like fish. A seed grows under each scale. When the seeds are fully grown, the scales open, and the seeds fall out.

How do squirrels and other animals stay warm in winter?

Animals stay warm in all different ways. Most animals' fur gets thicker as the weather becomes cold. And many of them try to stay inside their dens as much as possible.

Birds fluff up their feathers and try to stay out of the wind.

Opossums sleep for days on end in hollow logs or burrows when it's cold.

Garter snakes burrow together below the ground to hibernate through the winter.

Woodchucks, or **groundhogs**, eat a lot in the summer. Then they hibernate. They sleep until spring, when they get hungry again.

In the winter, **squirrels** sleep in cozy squirrel nests that they make high in the treetops. They don't go outside much at all.

Raccoons sleep almost all the time in their homes in hollow trees.

Chipmunks sleep most of the winter, too.

45

How will I know when it is spring?

In the spring, the weather turns warmer. If there's snow, it melts, and the sun shines longer each day. Birds who left for the winter return and build nests for eggs. Animals who slept all winter creep from burrows with their newborn babies. Tiny leaves sprout on trees, plants and flowers begin to grow, and the whole world seems suddenly green again.

TIME-LIFE for CHILDREN ®

Assistant Managing Editor: Patricia Daniels
Editorial Directors: Jean Burke Crawford, Allan Fallow,
Karin Kinney, Sara Mark, Elizabeth Ward
Publishing Assistant: Marike van der Veen
Production Manager: Marlene Zack
Senior Copyeditor: Colette Stockum
Production: Celia Beattie
Supervisor of Quality Control: James King
Assistant Supervisor of Quality Control: Miriam Newton
Library: Louise D. Forstall

Special Contributor: Barbara Klein
Researcher: Eugenia Scharf
Writer: Jacqueline A. Ball

Designed by: **David Bennett Books**

Series design: David Bennett
Book design: Andrew Crowson
Art direction: David Bennett & Andrew Crowson
Illustrated by: Malcolm Livingstone
Additional cover
illustrations by: Malcolm Livingstone

©1993 Time Life Inc. All rights reserved.
No part of this book may be reproduced in any form or by any electronic or mechanical means, including information
storage and retrieval devices or systems, without prior written permission from the publisher, except that brief
passages may be quoted for reviews.

First printing. Printed in U.S.A.
Published simultaneously in Canada.

Time Life Inc. is a wholly owned subsidiary of THE TIME INC. BOOK COMPANY.

TIME-LIFE is a trademark of Time Warner Inc. U.S.A.

For subscription information, call 1-800-621-7026.

Library of Congress Cataloging-in-Publication Data

Why is the grass green? : first questions and answers about nature.
p. cm.— (Time-Life library of first questions and answers)
Summary : Answers questions about the natural world, including "Why
do dandelions get fuzzy?" "Why do bees buzz around flowers?" and
"How do birds fly?"
ISBN 0-7835-0858-1 (trade).— ISBN (invalid) 0-7835-0859-1 (lib. bdg.)
1. Natural history— Miscellanea--Juvenile literature. 2. Plants--
—Miscellanea--Juvenile Literature. 3. Animals--Miscellanea —
—Juvenile Literature. 4. Nature--Miscellanea--Juvenile Literature.
[1. Nature--Miscellanea. 2. Natural history--Miscellanea.
3. Questions and answers.] I. Time-Life for Children (Firm)
II. Series: Library of first questions and answers.
QH48.W447 1993
574 — dc20   93-17372
                                                                              CIP
                                                                              AC

Consultants

Dr. Lewis P. Lipsitt, an internationally recognized specialist on childhood development, was the 1990 recipient of the Nicholas Hobbs Award for science in the service of children. He has served as the science director for the American Psychological Association and is a professor of psychology and medical science at Brown University, where he is director of the Child Study Center.

Thomas D. Mullin directs the Hidden Oaks Nature Center in Fairfax County, Virginia, where he coordinates workshops and seminars designed to promote appreciation for wildlife and the environment. He is also the Washington representative for the National Association for Interpretation, a professional organization for naturalists involved in public education.

Dr. Judith A. Schickedanz, an authority on the education of preschool children, is an associate professor of early childhood education at the Boston University School of Education, where she also directs the Early Childhood Learning Laboratory. Her published work includes *More Than the ABC's: Early Stages of Reading and Writing Development* as well as several textbooks and many scholarly papers.